T0154193

INSPIRATION

for the Soul

Also in this series:
Inspiration for the Heart

INSPIRATION

for the Soul

KATE MARR KIPPENBERGER

EXISLE
PUBLISHING

First published as *Soul Food: Recipes for a Happier Life* 2005
This edition published 2015

Exisle Publishing Limited,
'Moonrising', Narone Creek Road, Wollombi,
NSW 2325, Australia
P.O. Box 60-490, Titirangi, Auckland 0642, New Zealand
www.exislepublishing.com

A CiP record for this book is available from the
National Library of Australia.

ISBN 978 1 921966 89 7

Text design and production by BookNZ
Cover design by Dexter Fry
Printed in China

This book uses paper sourced under ISO 14001 guidelines
from well-managed forests and other controlled sources.

10 9 8 7 6 5 4 3 2 1

Perspective

Sometimes we react to things disproportionately to their importance. When something has just happened, it may be difficult to put it in perspective because our feelings seem very powerful. Yet we know from past experience that in a couple of days we're unlikely to feel so strongly about it. To gain this perspective in the moment ask yourself, 'Will this matter in a year's/month's/week's time?'. It probably won't, so why worry about it now?

Listening

When someone is talking to you, concentrate solely on what's being said, rather than asking yourself 'What's in it for me?' or 'What does this mean for me?'. Such thoughts can detract from the relationships we have with others. At that point you're simply there to listen. If you engage fully in listening to others, your relationships improve.

Solitude

To truly know ourselves we need to spend time alone. Many of us find solitude with no external stimulation boring because we are accustomed to filling our time with work, sport, watching TV or socialising. While these activities may be important, we all need balance in our lives. Allow yourself quiet time alone to get to know who you really are.

Significant Others

Fostering meaningful relationships
is one of the best ways to feed your
soul. Most of us have meaningful
relationships with only a few people
because it takes time and effort to
build and maintain close relationships.
Think of these people as your
'significant others'. Why worry what
a 'non-significant other' thinks?
Your time is precious, so be aware of
how you use it.

Happiness

Rather than focusing on what makes you happy, think about what happiness is. Most of us imagine that happiness will come when we achieve certain goals. But happiness isn't reliant on external factors – it is totally within us. We create our own happiness every moment by our attitude towards ourselves and the world around us. If you expect true happiness to arrive only when you achieve your goals, you may be disappointed as it may always elude you. However, if you realise that you can create happiness, it has the potential to be with you always.

Responsibility

It's important to be honest enough with ourselves to take responsibility for all outcomes we had a part in creating, whether good or bad. Some people take credit for all things good, and blame others for all things bad, while others do the very opposite. Neither of these scenarios is likely to be true for anyone. We are each responsible for some good and some negative experiences in our lives. We should feel good about ourselves for the positive experiences, and reflect on the wisdom we gained from the negative ones.

Relationships

The best relationships exist when each partner allows the other to grow. This might mean spending time alone or participating in hobbies the other partner doesn't share. If each partner is able to grow and develop as an individual then the relationship benefits enormously.

When problems arise in a relationship, it's very easy to run away by ending the relationship. Yet every issue that confronts us gives us an opportunity to learn about ourselves and others. If we run away, we learn very little. If we end the relationship without learning how to effectively resolve the problems, we may face the same problems in future relationships. Healthy relationships where problems arise and are resolved are very fulfilling.

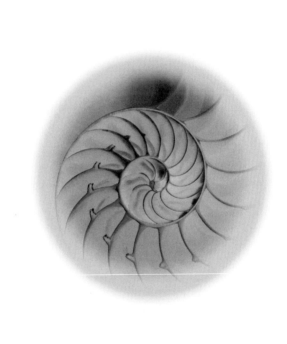

Reactions

There are times when we find
ourselves at the receiving end of
someone's anger or frustration, and we
imagine they're directing this emotion
at us. The reality is that their reaction
isn't about us at all, but about them.
If someone is angry about something
you did, listen for any truths and take
the lesson. But remember that their
reaction is a reflection of themselves
and there's no need for you to take
it personally.

Advice

Don't be afraid to ask for and accept advice from others. We tend to see our own concerns from our own limited perspective. Asking for advice means you're willing to consider a new perspective, which will be more objective than your own. It may even provide a clarity that you've been unable to reach on your own.

Truth

Be true to yourself. Do things because you want to do them, not to please someone else. Sometimes being true to ourselves means standing up for something we believe in, or speaking up when previously we might have said nothing for fear of a negative reaction. We owe it to ourselves to be guided by our convictions.

Change

Accept that change is inevitable.
We can choose either to accept
change or resist it and suffer the
consequences. Change provides us
with many lessons and opportunities
for growth. Even though we might
be pushed out of our comfort zone
and required to do something in a
different way, this doesn't mean that
things will take a turn for the worse.
The learning available to you as a
result of change can improve your life.
Have faith that things will turn out well.

Feelings

The feeling of being taken advantage of is powerful for some. It's a feeling that someone has crossed our line of fairness. As a result, we may feel negatively towards them, which may transform into guilt for us. If you find yourself in this situation, be honest about your feelings. The effects of not being honest with other people are far worse than the effect honesty has on them. A relationship might be saved by honesty, but without it the relationship is bound to suffer.

Souls

We are all human beings with souls. If we see loving, kind and caring behaviour in someone we are glimpsing their soul. If we see anger, irrationality and jealousy it doesn't mean that person is without a loving soul, it just means that they are keeping it well hidden. If someone behaves badly towards you, they are probably very unhappy in themselves. Until we can act from our highest self, which is loving and compassionate, we affect our own happiness.

Priorities

Spend time today thinking about your life priorities. Are you supporting your priorities by the amount of time you're allocating to them? Consider the following: family, health, happiness and money. Which of these is most important to you? If you didn't put happiness first, you may be setting yourself up for the scenario 'I'll be happy when ...'. Making happiness conditional upon achieving something means it can come and go depending on circumstances. Happiness is only dependent on how you choose to think at any given time. It is possible to be happy without one, two or even three of the above factors. If you make being happy your top priority, you're more likely to achieve it.

Communication

We tend to behave in a way we would like others to behave towards us, and communicate in the way we would like others to communicate with us. However, without understanding this about ourselves, and with everyone around us doing the same thing, there are likely to be misunderstandings. In a relationship it's important to communicate to each other how you like to be treated. For it is only then that you can each give and receive what you need.

Respect

Treat every living thing with respect, as all things have an important role to play and a right to live in peace. Being cruel to animals or to each other does not feed the soul. In fact it's an aspect of ourselves on which we should reflect. Why not show respect when every living thing deserves it?

Worry

Don't worry about anything that is beyond your control because you can't do anything about it, and worrying will only cause you unnecessary stress. Why allow yourself to stress over something you can't control? Worrying is simply wasting energy. Examine your worries today and decide whether to forget them because they're beyond your control or settle on a plan of action to deal with those within your control.

Language

The language we use impacts on our wellbeing. Take the word 'should', for example. By saying to ourselves that we 'should' do something, we're giving ourselves no freedom of choice.

To make life easier for yourself, try replacing the word 'should' with 'could'. If you don't do something you 'could' have done, it doesn't matter so much because you weren't so strict on yourself to begin with. Be aware of what you tell others they 'should' do too, as this creates added pressure for them.

Breathing

Spend some time today concentrating on your breathing. Breathing deeply not only keeps you alive, but it improves the way you feel. Increasing the amount of oxygen in the body increases calmness and elevates the mood. So today, if you find yourself feeling stressed or low, take a few long, slow breaths and notice the improvement.

Giving

Today, try focusing not on what
you can do for yourself, but on
what you can do for someone else.
It can be quite refreshing to consider
someone else's needs for a change.
Your gesture does not need to be
huge, but simply come from your heart.
Some of the most powerful gestures
go unnoticed by the recipient.
Such gestures are powerful because
they weren't motivated by a desire
for recognition, but by a desire to
benefit someone else. So today, think
of something nice you can do for
another person, and notice how it
makes you feel.

Animal Energy

In our busy lives filled with family, work and friends we sometimes forget the calming and healing benefits associated with stroking and cuddling our pets. The energy we gain from a pet's unconditional love is enormous. So today, allow yourself uninterrupted time with your pet and appreciate the sense of calm and healing energy it gives you.

Battles

There may be some things worth fighting for, but there are many situations where fighting is a waste of energy. It's important to stand up for your beliefs when they're being threatened, not just because someone doesn't share your views. Battling with others in the hope they'll adopt your beliefs could put a strain on your relationships. If you wish others to respect your beliefs, you need to respect the beliefs of others.

Frustration

The people in your life can teach you a lot about yourself. You can either learn the lessons, or remain disappointed and frustrated by other people's behaviour. The things that frustrate you about someone else say more about you. The annoying behaviours you notice in others are actually reflections of issues you have within yourself – other people are not necessarily frustrated by these behaviours. Whenever you have a negative reaction to another person's behaviour ask yourself, 'Why did I react that way?'.

Stimulation

There's a saying that if we eliminated all stress from our lives we'd be dead. The stress response was designed to save our lives in the face of an immediate threat, not to be an everyday occurrence. Perhaps then we could say that it's important to have stimulation in our lives, rather than stress. So instead of accepting stress, accept healthy levels of stimulation.

Fear

Fear can drive negative behaviours and create negative consequences for us. It may be a fear of being alone, a fear of failure, or a fear of death. We may not be aware of the fear, but subconsciously it exerts control. So, if you catch yourself behaving in a negative manner and you're not getting the results you want, ask yourself, 'What am I afraid of here?'. It may be that you can put that fear to rest.

Beliefs

The beliefs you have about yourself play a significant role in the life you lead. How successful do you think you could be? How wealthy do you think you could be? How happy do you think you could be? If you believe you won't be successful, wealthy or happy then you won't be. If you believe you could be very successful, wealthy and happy then you'll achieve those goals to a far greater extent.

Ability

Remember that everyone does their best with what they have, in terms of their skills, knowledge and abilities. Generally people don't go out of their way to upset or annoy us. The fact that they might not behave according to our expectations doesn't mean we should judge them negatively. If we choose to believe that a person is doing their best rather than getting upset or annoyed with them, we create positive energy for ourselves and others.

Self-Love

The most important thing you can do is love yourself for who you are right now. Don't put it off until you're more patient, thinner, less irritable, more loving or whatever it is you want to improve about yourself. The fact is you are not and will never be perfect. The things you're dealing with are necessary for your learning and growth, so embrace them and love yourself for who you are right now. You might even find the things you don't like about yourself will take care of themselves.

Nourishment

In order to live in the present and appreciate what is happening to us at this moment, we need to slow down. This is particularly important when we're eating. When we eat slowly and stay in the present moment, we allow ourselves to savour every mouthful and gain maximum nourishment from our food. So today, slow down and concentrate on your eating and you'll be healthier on all levels.

Order

One of the ways you can create calmness for yourself is to make sure that you're not surrounded by chaos and mess, as disarray creates tension in your life. So today, concentrate on cleaning up anything that is disorderly or cluttered around you, be it your workplace, your bedroom, your workshop or your kitchen. It's far easier to attain a state of calmness when you've cleared the clutter!

Calm

Say to yourself, 'Whatever today brings, I'm going to handle it in a calm and considered way'. Taking time to consider your reactions means you are more likely to be effective in your responses and more able to appreciate the moment. We tend to 'see' more when we are less emotional in our reactions, with the result that we gain more from each moment.

Getting There

Rather than spending time thinking
about the goals you have or the
outcomes you want, focus on how
you're going to achieve them.
If you focus only on the goals you
have set yourself, you are limiting
the possibilities available to you.
If you focus on the process to achieve
your goals, it may lead you to
outcomes or a destination that far
exceed your current thinking.

Learning

Every person, circumstance or event, whether it is positive or not so positive, teaches you something about yourself. Rather than spending time dwelling on things that have happened in the past, think about the things you have learnt about yourself as a result. Your past experiences have made you the person you are today. Dwelling on things that have happened is a waste of your precious time. The moment has passed, but your learning remains.

Empowerment

Spend some time today thinking about what makes you happy. Focus on specific things that you can do because you have the sole responsibility for your happiness. The knowledge that you have the power to do whatever it takes to make you happy is very empowering. If you spend time considering what you can do to make yourself happy right now, you'll be able to treat yourself whenever you need to.

Gratitude

Consider the things you are thankful for. It's impossible to feel negative when you give thanks for the things you have. Grateful people find more and more to be thankful for, whereas negative people find more and more to whinge about. If you have an 'abundance mentality', you attract more positive things to you; if you have a 'scarcity mentality', the opposite is true. So consciously develop an abundance mentality today, and start by giving thanks for what you have.

Tolerance

Be tolerant of the differences you see in other people. We all live according to our own beliefs and values, so everyone is different. Our reactions to these differences teach us about ourselves, especially if we find we become annoyed. If we fail to learn what it is within us that makes us annoyed, we will continue to encounter people who annoy us.

Stewing

There are times when people say or do things that we don't like or don't agree with. The worst thing to do is stew about it, as this creates negative energy and stress. You really have two choices: either you can tell the person how you feel and resolve the issue, or you can forget about it. If you dwell on things the only person who will suffer is you. So today, rather than stew, have the courage to talk about it, or the sense to forget it.

Expectations

One of the best ways to keep in control of your happiness is to reduce your expectations of others. Too often we allow ourselves to feel unhappy because someone didn't behave in the way we expected. The problem with expectations is that most of the time others are unaware of them, and if people happen to behave in a way consistent with them, it's probably due to chance. Therefore we must enable family and friends to live their lives free from our expectations, and we should live free from theirs. Today consider any expectations you have. Think to yourself, 'if this happens, it will be nice, but I'm not going to expect it.'

Talent

We have each been blessed with the possession of a special gift or talent. By using this gift, no matter what it is, you will make the world a better place. Your gift will be something you love doing. If you find yourself unhappy at work, it might be because you're not getting the opportunity to use your gift. If it's not possible to use your gift in the workplace, make the most of it in your free time. If you spend more time using your gift, you will feel greater fulfilment in all aspects of your life.

Silence

Today allocate yourself some quiet time and regard it as your highest priority. Most of us get caught up in our busy lives and forget to take time for ourselves. Make sure you'll be free from interruptions. When you're enjoying your quiet time, pay attention to slowing down and calming your thoughts, then appreciate the silence. Quiet time provides you with much needed balance in a hectic day, and restores a sense of calm.

Wishing

One of the most damaging thoughts we can have is wishing that things were different. Why deny yourself happiness right now by thinking, 'I'll be happy when ...'? If you think like that, happiness will elude you because you'll always find something else to wish for in the future. Your happiness will never come. Today tell yourself that life is fine the way it is, and the only thing that affects it is your perception.

Courage

From today, concentrate on doing things that feel right for you. You are the only person who can determine this for yourself, yet it's easy to find yourself doing things because you think you 'should', or worrying about what others will think. It takes courage to do what's right for yourself yet it is only by doing this that you can attain true happiness. You will never be happy if you overlook your own needs to satisfy the wishes of others.

Direction

Life is a journey with many crossroads. There are times when we find ourselves at a junction where we struggle to make a decision about which direction to take because we're fearful of the outcome. There's no time to fear the outcome if you focus on the next step of the journey. Focus on the next step and your path may suddenly become clear.

Problems

It's important to deal with any issues in your life causing you unhappiness. One reason we may choose not to deal with our problems is because we are accustomed to having that problem in our lives and feeling unhappy. Or we might be afraid of what could be uncovered when the issue is explored. These excuses not to act stem from fear, but it is worth facing our fears to make ourselves happy.

Goals

We are conditioned to set goals, aim high and expect the best.

It's important to understand why you're aiming for a particular goal. How will achieving this goal create happiness? Will you be content when you achieve that goal, or will you continue striving for more? Why? Understanding the answers to these questions will not only help you to achieve your goals, but will increase the likelihood that your goals will bring you happiness.

Changes

Everyone has the ability and the right to change. It's very unlikely we will stay the same, with the same attitudes, values and behaviour for our entire lives. For some people changes occur slowly and are barely obvious, yet for others remarkable changes can occur in a short period of time. We must learn to accept change and ensure we don't deny it in our own lives or the lives of others, thereby inhibiting personal growth.

Vocation

There is a saying, 'Do what you love and you'll have what you need'. Too often we wind up in jobs we dislike to support an unfulfilling lifestyle. We live in a society that portrays success as achieving wealth and all its trappings. The problem is that people unconsciously subscribe to this without considering whether it's right for them. If you do what you love, you will be able to support a lifestyle that makes you happy. You might not be a millionaire, but your life can still be very fulfilling.

Lightening Up

Today think about lightening up instead of carrying the weight of the world on your shoulders. Begin by focusing solely on the day ahead. Don't worry about what happened yesterday or what might happen tomorrow. Your load will be much lighter if you just focus on what you need to do today. Make sure that what you hope to achieve today is realistic. After all, it is just one day. At the end of the day reflect on how lightening up affected your mood.

Burdens

Too often we focus on the burdens in our lives and wish they would go away. Problems are here to teach us something about ourselves. If we put in the effort to overcome our burdens, by either removing them from our lives, or changing the way we think about them, the satisfaction we'll feel will far outweigh the effort exerted. So make a choice to deal with a burden in your life, and decide what it will take to overcome it, realising that any effort will be more than rewarded with a greater sense of achievement.

Unconditional Love

The ultimate feeling we can experience is to give and receive unconditional love. Unconditional love means loving someone or something no matter what they do, for example, loving your partner even though they've just said something hurtful, or loving your cat or dog even after they've destroyed your favourite plant. Today examine your ideas about love and see whether you're creating conditions for yourself and others such as 'I'll be loved if I lose weight' or 'I'll love him if he remembers my birthday' and start practising unconditional love. Take the time to notice the effect it has on you and those around you.

Reflection

We often become so immersed in
our busy lives that we forget to stop,
take a step back and have an objective
look at ourselves. It's a good habit to
reflect, because we not only identify
if there's a need to make any
changes, but we also notice our
achievements and our great qualities.
Today, reflect on three characteristics
you love about yourself, and make a
conscious effort to remind yourself of
these things often. Take note of how
you feel at the end of the day.

Dreams

It's easy to talk yourself out of following your dreams by telling yourself things like 'I don't have the skills', 'I'm too old' or 'No one like me has ever achieved this before'. Such beliefs are self-fulfilling prophecies. If you have a dream, you owe it to yourself to pursue it.

The Past

Try to keep the past in perspective. Accept that dealing with issues from the past can take time, but don't let them hold you captive and prevent you from enjoying today. Your past has played a very important role because it has brought you to where you are today, but it does not need to dictate your future. At this moment, there are a huge number of choices open to you, yet you may fail to see them because you are looking through the eyes of your past. For example, spending years at university studying for a particular career doesn't mean you are tied to that field forever. It has brought you to today. What you do from here is up to you.

Control

Remember that you are in control of your life. Our internal dialogues can have a powerful impact. For example, don't tell yourself you'll only have one cup of coffee today if you know you'll end up having more, because you're effectively telling yourself that you're not in control. Set yourself achievable goals so you feel in control.

Focus

It's beneficial to spend a little time each day by yourself, free from interruptions and free from intruding thoughts. Listen to your favourite piece of music. Think about the melody, the beat, the lyrics and the vocals for the entire piece, and lose yourself in the enjoyment it brings you. If you find other thoughts intruding, gently push them aside and refocus. When the song is finished notice how revitalised you feel.

Mindset

Whatever your mindset, you create
and attract things to you that are
consistent with your thoughts.
If you have a positive mindset, you
will see the world in a positive way,
and because of your positive energy,
you will attract wonderful experiences.
Being in a negative frame of mind
prevents us from experiencing anything
positive. So today, think about your
mindset, and try your best to maintain
a positive one.

Interpretation

Our behaviour is a reflection of how we feel, and one of the ways we communicate with others. However, the chance of someone else correctly interpreting your behaviour is low because no two minds are alike. So if you rely on your behaviour to get your message across, be prepared for others to misinterpret it. If you want someone to know what you're thinking or feeling, tell them!

Going Solo

Today plan an activity that you can do by yourself. We tend to think that there are certain experiences we should share with others. Why not try some of these activities solo? When you do something by yourself, you enjoy the experience internally, rather than discussing it with someone else at the time. Going solo can be challenging if you're unaccustomed to it. However, enjoying activities with only yourself for company feeds the soul and shows you that there's no need to be lonely.

Striving

Sometimes we find ourselves striving for something we have great difficulty attaining. If you find yourself in this situation, stop trying so hard!

The desperate energy created by constant striving may be pushing the desired outcome away. How many times have you heard of someone desperately searching for a partner who only crosses their path when they've given up the search? Today, relax around the things you're striving for. If it's meant to happen, it will be taken care of.

Forgiveness

Being able to forgive is an essential life
skill. The only person who suffers
when you hold a grudge is you
because you are the one harbouring
the negative thoughts and feelings.
The act of forgiving allows you to free
your mind of all the negative thoughts
around that circumstance. The person
you find hardest to forgive is the
person you most need to forgive.
Just make the decision to forgive and
it will be taken care of.

Lessons

If you find yourself continually dealing with the same tricky circumstance or difficult type of person, consider this to be one of your lessons. If you pass up the opportunity to learn the lesson, you will continue to be faced with these circumstances. Once you've accepted what there is to learn you'll notice how these difficulties begin to disappear from your life.

Assumptions

We must never presume to know what someone else is thinking. There are times when we see people reacting negatively and imagine it's due to something we did. This belief creates a negative reaction in us and we might start thinking things like, 'How dare they react like that when I was just ...!' The reality of the situation might not be as we imagine.

Remember that assumptions are nothing more than your interpretation of events.

Points of View

Be mindful of the fact that every person you come into contact with today will have a different perspective to yours. Even those people who agree with you will have a different perspective because they're looking at the same situation through different eyes. Today, make an effort to understand others' points of view first, then explain your own for their understanding. This approach will add value to all of your interactions.

Self-Belief

The belief you have in yourself will be the major determinant of your life accomplishments. If you believe you can accomplish a lot, you will. If you believe you can accomplish very little, you will. If there's something you would like to accomplish but you're having trouble believing you can do it, break it down into smaller more achievable chunks. As you achieve these smaller chunks you will not only feel great about your achievements, but you will be closer to reaching your goal. By achieving what you can today, your belief in yourself will grow for tomorrow.

Positive Thoughts

Thoughts are a form of energy that affect the world around us, contributing either to negative energy or positive energy. So today, send out thoughts that make the world a better place. Imagine them spreading around the world and positively affecting people you don't even know. Imagine what the world would be like if everyone concentrated on sending out positive thoughts.

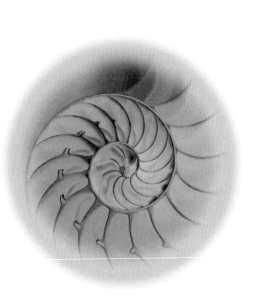

Pace

The pace at which we move through our lives has a direct relationship to the way we feel. I don't mean how pressured you feel or the number of things you have to do, but how you move and express yourself. Those people who always move quickly, have very expressive gestures, and talk faster and louder than most are less likely to feel relaxed. You can feel relaxed in your day-to-day activities by slowing down your movements and consciously relaxing your gestures and expressions, including your speech. Try this today and notice how relaxed you feel.

Standards

We all have standards we set ourselves for various aspects of our lives. We know what sort of spouse, parent, worker, friend or team member we'd like to be. It's important from time to time to review these standards so we don't set them so high we can't reach them. In every moment we must try our best and be content with the result. If our best doesn't allow us to reach our expectations, we will never be content and happy with ourselves. So today, examine your standards and make sure they can be achieved by doing your best.

Moods

As humans our moods are constantly changing. We tend to think life is great when we're in a good mood, and awful when we're in a low mood. The reality is that your life doesn't suddenly decline or improve at these times; the only thing that changes is your perspective. Therefore, it's important to take your thoughts less seriously in a low mood, and realise they are only a consequence of your mood. Today, if you find yourself in a low mood, see it for what it is, and give yourself a break from thinking.

Anticipation

Too often we find ourselves spending time worrying about things that might happen. This is pointless for many reasons. Firstly, it takes our attention away from the present moment. Secondly, our future will either be in our control or beyond our control. Either way, we don't need to worry. Thirdly, worrying creates negative energy that harms us on every level. Finally, the reality is that most of what we worry about doesn't happen, and if something does, we deal with it just fine. So stop worrying today!

Struggle

Life is not meant to be a constant struggle. If you are always struggling and running into 'roadblocks' or you're finding it very difficult to achieve your goals, then the things you're striving for might not be meant for you.

In this case, re-evaluate your situation and either change your goals, or change the way you approach them. We all face hurdles in order to learn and grow, but life shouldn't be full of hurdles.

Self-Reliance

Rather than relying on others for emotional support, if we make ourselves the primary source of love and support, then we become whole. Too often we go through rough patches, then rely on someone else to build us up again. This is a risky strategy because one day there might not be anyone else to build us up. The next time you face a difficult time, make sure the thoughts you have about yourself are kind and loving. You'll find it much easier to get through the situation.

Competition

We live in a very competitive world. However, if you are competitive in your relationships with significant others, you are doing yourself an injustice. Examples of competitive behaviour include always wanting to be right or wanting 'more' than your significant other. For you to be a winner in a competitive situation, your significant other (who is presumably someone you care about) has to lose. How can you win by making someone you care about lose? So today, think about whether you're trying to compete with someone you care about, and decide whether it's worth it.

Compassion

It's very easy to fall into the trap of reacting to other people's behaviour. If someone is rude to us, or if an impatient driver cuts us off in the street, we become annoyed. Instead of feeling annoyed, try to feel compassion by putting yourself in their shoes. Imagine how bad you'd feel to be rude to another person, or how stressed you would feel to be in such a hurry. By taking the focus away from yourself, you realise that other people potentially have problems worse than your own, so be thankful for what you have.

Knowing

Each of us knows what's right for us.
Others can give their opinion, but only
we can know for sure. If we are filled
with desperation, emotion or fear, the
quiet part of us that does know will not
be heard. The best way to uncover
what is right for you is to spend some
quiet time focusing on controlling your
thoughts and calming your emotions
so you can hear that quiet inner voice
that is your intuition.

Stress

While we've all heard that some stress is beneficial to us, this is only true if we're about to 'perform'. Stress produces adrenaline in our bodies to elevate our performance for a short time. This was useful for our ancestors who faced life-threatening situations from which they needed to escape.

However, these days most of our stress is created by the anticipation of something going wrong, not by an immediate threat. But the brain doesn't discriminate and so adrenaline is produced just by imagining a bad scenario. If you find yourself stressed over a particular thought process, go for a walk rather than allowing those thoughts to build up. By recognising and dealing with stress this way, the effects are less likely to accumulate.

Power

If you're in a situation where someone is intentionally trying to upset or bully you, the way you respond to them determines who has the power. No matter what anyone is trying to do to you, they have no control over how you respond. If you don't allow them to affect you, they have absolutely no power over you. However, if you react negatively to them, they will see they're having an effect on you and probably continue with the behaviour. So today, remind yourself 'no one has the power to make me feel bad'.

Reality

How much time do you spend thinking about what you want in life? Most of the time we're actually looking for the feeling associated with achieving or acquiring a particular thing.

When we look at it this way, we can see that our focus might be on the wrong thing, and that concentrating on how we feel is most important. Once we recognise this it can be liberating because there is likely to be more than one way to achieve the feeling, whereas there may be only one way to achieve the thing. In fact, you might be able to achieve the feeling today!

Self-Talk

How we talk to ourselves defines how others see and react to us. If we constantly say things to ourselves like 'I'm lazy', 'I'm incapable of achieving that' or 'I'm not bright/creative/funny enough', we prevent ourselves from reaching our full potential. However, if we focus on our great qualities – and we all have them – we empower ourselves to reach our full potential. Today, pay attention to any negative statements you make to yourself, then replace each negative one with something positive.

Cheerfulness

Sometimes we make ourselves feel happy by the things we do. If you feel unhappy, alter your mood by talking more cheerfully, using more cheerful words and relaxing your facial muscles into a smile. You'll be amazed at how easy it is to feel happy and cheerful by tricking the mind into believing it's cheerful. So today, if you find yourself feeling anything other than cheerful, modify your outward behaviour and see what effect this has.

Appreciation

So much of our effort is spent influencing the way things happen. We spend a lot of time thinking about the outcomes we desire and trying to make them happen. Yet so little time is spent appreciating the results when we achieve them, no matter how small they might be; it's almost as if we take them for granted. So today, spend some time focusing on and appreciating the positive outcomes you've worked hard to achieve before progressing to the next goal.

Doing Your Best

Today make a conscious effort to do your absolute best in everything you do. If you do your best no one can criticise you, and most of all you can't criticise yourself. Even if something doesn't go according to plan, or you do not achieve an outcome you were expecting, if you know in your heart you did your best, then whatever happens is meant to be.

Recognition

Sometimes we focus so intently on what we want to achieve that we forget to recognise the good things that other people do. With a little bit of effort you can make someone else feel acknowledged, which in turn will have a positive effect on you. So today, take the time to recognise someone else for something they do well, whether it's the cleaner, your boss or the person at the supermarket checkout, and then tell them what a good job they're doing. Don't forget to spend some time enjoying their reaction.

Mondays

Sometimes we find ourselves thinking negatively about something because that seems to be the way everyone else thinks about it. For instance, why don't we like Mondays as much as Fridays? Most of us feel low on Monday because the weekend has come to an end. Yet Mondays signify the beginning of another week full of opportunity and potentially fantastic experiences, all within our control. And when you think about it, Friday signifies the end of yet another week in our precious life. So let's make the most of it by enjoying every day!

Laughter

Laughing is one of the best ways to make yourself feel good. On a physical level, laughing releases endorphins that give us a sense of happiness. On a mental level, laughter occurs when we think about something positive or remember happy times. Laughing can increase our energy levels and thereby increase the positive energy that radiates from us to others. If nothing funny happens to you today, spend some time recalling something that made you laugh and enjoy that moment all over again.

Nutrition

Take note of what you eat. The chemicals in foods we eat have different effects on us. As a general rule of thumb, heavy or convenience foods deflate our mood, while nutritious foods such as fruit and vegetables improve our mood. So today concentrate on the foods you eat and how you feel after eating them. This will give you an incentive to stick to the foods that make you feel good.

Time Management

Be rigorous in determining whether the tasks you have to do today are achievable or a waste of your time. Too often we plough into our day without much thought or planning, and sometimes we work in a particular way because it's the way we've always done it. It is harder to attain true happiness when you're flat out doing things. So today concentrate your energy on the things that are achievable.

The Present

Living in the present moment is one of the most powerful things we can do to feed the soul. If you're thinking about what might happen tomorrow, or what happened yesterday, you're missing out on what life offers right now. By limiting our focus to the present moment we exclude certain habitual thoughts that have the potential to make us unhappy. To live in the present moment, focus your attention on every detail of whatever you're doing right now. Notice the way things look, smell, sound and feel. Be aware of any expectations you create, and see them as a signal to focus on the present.

Non-Significant Others

We don't ever need to worry about what 'non-significant others' are thinking about us, because we probably don't figure in their thinking. They're thinking about themselves and worrying about what others are thinking of them! Most of our 90 000 thoughts in a day centre around ourselves; what we have to do, what we look like, how we feel and so on. How much time would you spend thinking about what someone wore to a party, or how someone looked in the supermarket, or the mistake someone made at work? My guess is minimal time, and it's the same for everyone else. Realise this, and notice how liberated you begin to feel.

Thoughts

We feel happy when we have positive thoughts and unhappy when we have negative thoughts, therefore our happiness is a direct result of our thoughts. Our thoughts are completely within our control, so we always have a choice to consider a situation positively or negatively. We tend to think it is the situation that affects our happiness, but it is how we think about the situation that affects our mood. So today, be aware of your thoughts with respect to any negative situation.

Make a choice to think about the situation in a different light, and notice the effect it has on your happiness.

Discontentment

Learning to accept things as they are feeds the soul. By not accepting something, you're effectively wishing it was different, or waiting for it to be different in the future, which takes away from happiness in the present moment. Even if a situation is not ideal, accept it, and in doing so you will reduce any negative feelings and be able to deal with it in a more effective way.

Imagination

In order to realise our potential we need imagination. Imagination allows us to think about and recognise all sorts of possibilities and opportunities. Without imagination we're stuck with what we know, and may spend our lives doing the same old things, and missing out on opportunities for new experiences. If you use your imagination, you're allowing yourself to be open to the infinite number of possibilities that exist for us all.

Intuition

Your intuition is the most powerful tool at your disposal. It is the internal guide that will never lead you astray. The voice of your intuition is quieter and more subtle than your normal internal dialogue. Anything it wants to 'tell' you will come as a sense of knowing rather than in words. To tap into your inner wisdom, practise quietening your thoughts right down. You will need to persevere, but the benefits are worth it.

Inhibitions

Sometimes we miss opportunities that are meant for us because of our inhibiting thoughts. If deep down inside you know there's a path you'd like to take, allow yourself some time to identify the thoughts that are preventing you from taking this path. Consider each thought and come up with an alternative perspective – one that isn't limiting. Too often we give our thoughts more power than is really warranted.

Living Courageously

We all have enough courage inside us to follow the right path. Some people choose to take an easy road rather than put in the effort to lead a more fulfilling life. Others know that by being courageous and facing situations that take them out of their comfort zone, they'll end up experiencing more and feeling more fulfilled. So trust that you have nothing to lose and everything to gain by choosing to live courageously.

Out of Sorts

Give yourself permission to feel out of sorts occasionally. The key thing is to recognise that you're out of sorts and perhaps to let others around you know this too. Sometimes we feel this way for no apparent reason, but dwelling on it won't help. Also, we might be inclined to act on this feeling if we think it's caused by someone else. This isn't a good idea. Give yourself a break, take care of yourself and know that the feeling will pass.

Nature

There is nothing more peaceful than sitting under a big tree gazing up at its branches, or walking on the beach watching the waves rolling in. It is easy to live in the moment when you're surrounded by natural beauty because there are so many wonderful things to look at, listen to, touch and smell. You'll find that by taking this time, appreciating the peace and living in the moment, your whole being will feel revitalised. You'll probably wonder why you don't do it more often.

Water

One of the best things you can do for your body is drink sufficient water to keep yourself hydrated. Without sufficient water your internal organs become stressed as they adapt to keep your body working. Today, focus on giving your body the water it needs and notice how much better you feel.

Success

What does success mean for you?
In our society symbols of success
such as a lucrative career, a nice
house and being married with a family
are seen as desirable. Some people
find themselves striving for these
things, only to find they are not happy
when they attain them. Think about
what will make you genuinely happy
and strive for that rather than society's
status symbols.

Needs

How much time each day do you spend doing something for yourself? You are the most important person in your life. No one else can attend to your needs as well as you can. No one else knows what's right for you at any given moment. It's up to you to identify your needs and what actions are required to attend to them. By taking responsibility for your own happiness, and not relying on others, you will free up other people to do the same.

Support

Sometimes we become entangled in other people's lives and problems. It's better to support others to deal with their own issues, rather than becoming involved. By getting involved, we may be affected by negative energy that ultimately saps us of the ability to support ourselves and our loved ones.

Listening

Effective listening is a valuable skill. By truly listening to another person you demonstrate that they are important, and by subsequently remembering details of conversations, you reinforce their importance. The opposite is true if you don't listen. So today, actively listen and notice the positive effects on those who talk to you.

Answers

When you have a problem to resolve,
sometimes the best strategy is to stop
thinking about it consciously.
Remember your intuition? It can assist
with any problem you're facing. By
'offering' the problem to your
subconscious to deal with, and having
faith that it will, you'll find the answers
to some of your most difficult problems.

Writing

Agonising over a problem clutters the mind with chaotic thoughts. If you continue like that, you'll be no closer to a solution and may feel frustration. To avoid this, organise your thoughts by writing them down. Once your thoughts are on paper you can take a more objective perspective. You'll see what makes sense and will be closer to finding a solution.

Exercise

Exercise benefits your physical, mental and spiritual wellbeing. It not only tones your muscles, burns fat and is good for your heart, it also makes you feel great. Exercise releases endorphins, which create a sense of wellbeing. Today allocate 20-30 minutes for exercise and notice how energised it makes you feel. Remember this feeling, and build exercise into your daily routine so that you can feel its benefits regularly.

Choice

Dwelling on the past is futile because you can't change what has already happened. We can't even change what happened five minutes ago! Rather than feeling dissatisfied with where you are now, recognise that the future will be whatever you choose to make it. Your future is not constrained by your past, unless you allow it to be.

Saying 'No'

Learn to say 'no' to the things you don't want to do. It doesn't mean you have to be rude, it simply means developing the courage to say 'no' in a polite but assertive way. If you say 'no' effectively, people understand, and if not, let the problem be theirs.

Breathing

Stress and tension are often associated with an increase in the speed of your breathing. This is your body's natural 'fight or flight' response. When in this situation, try concentrating on your breathing and consciously slowing it down to between five and ten breaths per minute. This will calm you down and put you in a better position to deal with the situation at hand.

Positivity

Our subconscious mind places no judgement on the thoughts we have. It works on the basis that whatever we're thinking must be true. So if you spend your time worrying about what might happen or imagining bad scenarios, your brain will flood your body with stress chemicals. Isn't it better to think about good things in your life and aim for more of them? Your thoughts are powerful and have a real impact on the life you live.

Appreciation

Think of someone you appreciate
having in your life and let them know
today. There are many times when we
appreciate the things people do, but
don't get around to telling them.
We may be afraid they'll think we're
'soppy' or as time passes we might
forget to show appreciation. Most of
us are not very practised at giving
or receiving compliments. So today,
tell someone you appreciate them, and
if it happens to you, accept the
compliment graciously.

Pets

Our pets can teach us a great deal about happiness. They exude contentment because they live in the moment. Pets don't think about what happened yesterday or what's going to happen tomorrow. They're happy in their own company and content to lie in the sun, yet they show us they also love having us around. Pets don't hold grudges – well, not for long. Giving them a pat, taking them for a walk and making sure they're well fed makes up for not being home all day. Don't underestimate your pet's ability to teach you about happiness.

Energy

We are essentially beings of energy. Energy flows into and out of us depending on what we're doing or thinking. The more energy we have the better we feel. Negative people try to increase their energy by taking from others, by putting others down and making them feel bad. The best way to improve your energy levels is to give positive feedback to the people around you and show them you appreciate them. They will enjoy your company and reflect positive energy towards you.

Irritability

Managing your stress levels is important if you want a long, happy and healthy life. For some people recognising their own stress is difficult, especially if they have been stressed for a long time. If we are continuously stressed, our body goes into a state of 'overdrive', creating wear and tear, which is unsustainable long term. Irritability is a primary symptom of stress. If you are irritable spend time thinking about the causes and identifying ways to manage them. Our natural state should be happiness, not irritability.

Comparisons

Comparing yourself to others is a futile exercise that will only make you unhappy. Imagining someone else's life is better than yours because they have things you envy, or because they seem to be free of your issues, is wasted energy. In reality they have their own problems, which they have as much trouble dealing with as you do your problems. So instead of comparing yourself to others, focus on making the most of your life.

An Open Mind

Just because you've always done something in a particular way doesn't mean that there are no alternatives. If we stick too rigidly to the way we've always done things, we may never move forward. Not being open-minded can leave us feeling stuck when it's really time to move on.

It is unlikely that a particular way of doing something will always be the best way, so don't let pride or stubbornness prevent you from discovering new possibilities.

Giving

The best way to ensure you receive the things you'd like to have is to give them to others first. If you want kindness, respect or love, then make sure you are giving these things out. Too often we resort to playing games so others will give us what we feel we need. For example, we might be angry because someone has not shown us love. By 'giving' anger, you can never receive the sort of love you desire, as a person's natural response to anger is not love. Be aware of what you need, and rather than playing games, try giving first.

Internal Voice

The greatest thing we each have to overcome is our own negative internal voice – the voice that says 'I can't do that' or 'What will they think of me?'. One tool you have to overcome this negative internal dialogue is discipline. If you decide to do something regardless of your negative internal voice, in time the negative inner voice will diminish, and self-defeating thoughts will be replaced by positive ones.

Habits

Our habits can hold us back from reaching our potential. Bad habits are generally things we wish we could stop, but we know it will take willpower and discipline. Start regarding your habits as within your control. Recognise that by 'kicking' one habit you can use the sense of achievement that follows to make progress in other areas of your life that also seem beyond your control.

Judgement

Today, be aware of any judgements you make or standards you impose on others. Just because someone doesn't behave the way we expect or doesn't reach our standards doesn't mean we should impose a judgement. Who are we to determine how others should behave? Also, it doesn't make sense to judge a person on their behaviour as we are generally unaware of their intentions. Very rarely do people act with bad intentions. So rather than creating negative energy for yourself by thinking badly about someone, be tolerant and compassionate.

Giving without Expectations

Today, give something without wanting anything in return. If you find yourself wanting something in return, you're taking away from the pleasure of giving, especially if you don't end up getting what you wanted! If you then feel disappointed and the recipient becomes aware of your disappointment, it is likely to undo the positive effect you created by giving. The gesture of giving isn't so loving if it's shrouded in expectation. Giving without expectations is a wonderful feeling for both the giver and the receiver.

'What If'

Don't worry about something that hasn't happened yet. Sometimes we create catastrophes about the way something might turn out. The mind can imagine no end of negative scenarios, so indulging in thoughts that typically begin with the phrase 'What if …' causes stress for no reason. Things are rarely as bad as we imagine, so 'catastrophising' wastes a lot of precious time and energy. Instead, try thinking, 'If the outcome is different from the one I hope for, I'll deal with it at the time'. Be aware of 'What if' thoughts today and don't indulge your worries.

Openness

Communication is the key to an effective relationship. If your partner does something that upsets you, talk to them about it in a calm and loving way rather than arguing. Bottling feelings up may create other problems in your relationship. By discussing the situation you may discover it wasn't your partner's intention to upset you.

Problems

Sometimes we make our problems larger than they really are by spending a lot of time thinking about them. For example, there may be a difficult person in your life who you have to see occasionally, and who you regard as a major problem because you spend so much time wishing they'd change.

A far healthier way to deal with this person is to think about them on the occasions you see them and forget about them the rest of the time.

Reactions

Stress is not something that happens to us – we create it by the way we react. This becomes clear when we see two people reacting to the same situation in different ways. We are responsible for our own reactions, yet we say things like 'He made me mad' or 'She stresses me out'. Whenever we're presented with a person or situation we can choose whether to let it affect us or not. This doesn't mean you have to put up with inappropriate behaviour, or bad situations. It just means you don't allow them to have a negative effect on you.

Peace

Try to remain at peace at all times, no matter what happens. By remaining at peace we retain control of a situation rather than allowing our emotions to control us. When we let our emotions control a situation it can escalate into something bigger than it really is, and we end up feeling bad. Most importantly, when at peace we allow ourselves to be guided by intuition. It's virtually impossible to hear this subtle internal 'voice' when we're emotional. So today, focus on remaining peaceful and notice the effects.

Early Mornings

Early morning can be the best part of the day, so try getting up early to make the most of it. Too often we make the excuse that we haven't got time for this and that, yet if we rearranged our day and gave ourselves an extra one or two hours in the morning, we could achieve a lot more. This can be time for yourself to do whatever you want to do. You could go for a walk, read or do some creative writing. The possibilities are endless!

Potential

If we believed in ourselves completely,
we would be capable of many things.
Most of us have varying degrees of
self-doubt that hold us back from
achieving our true potential. If
you're not achieving all you want,
consider how your thought patterns
may be contributing to the outcomes
you're receiving.

Self-Esteem

We all have talents as well as aspects of ourselves we can improve. Some people only focus on their negative attributes and are highly critical of themselves, whereas others focus on their assets without recognising opportunities to learn. It's important to continue to grow, but in doing so, we must recognise our qualities and the progress we've made so far.

History

Don't define someone by the way they have behaved in the past. Just because someone has behaved in a particular way until now doesn't mean they're going to behave that way next time. If you find yourself thinking, 'I can't say or do that because he/she will react like this', try being open-minded and you might be pleasantly surprised.

Christmas

Christmas can be a very stressful and unhappy time. Take some time to figure out what Christmas means to you. If it means stress, then it's worth examining why and attempting to eliminate that stress by doing something differently or considering things from a different perspective. As well as the tremendous religious and spiritual significance of Christmas, it's about love – whether it be for family, friends or ourselves. It's a time to reflect on the things most important to us. So try to eliminate any stress, and allow yourself to feel the true spirit of Christmas.

Memories

As we go through life we generate
memories for ourselves of people and
events that have positively influenced
us. These memories are powerful
and bring us comfort and happiness
when we think of them. They serve us
very well as situations change or
people are no longer in our lives.
Wouldn't it be nice to think that other
people's memories of us are also
positive, and give pleasure when we're
not around? Today, think about what
you can do to create a positive
memory for someone else.

Routine

By living your life strictly according to a routine you hamper your creativity and spontaneity, which may prevent you from reaching your potential. Instead of doing something just because it's a particular time of day and it is 'what you do', pay attention to your needs at any given moment, and act in accordance with them. Possibly your routine has no real meaning or benefit. Feed your soul by meeting your deepest needs at any given moment.

Colour

Appreciate the beauty around you.
We have been blessed with the natural
ability to see things in colour yet at
times we take this for granted.
Imagine a world where there was no
colour, then look around you at the
multitude of different colours you
can see. We are very lucky to be
able to see the array of colours in
nature. Spend some time appreciating
the beauty in the colours around
you today.

Honesty

One of the most important things you can do to feed your soul is to be honest with others about the way you're feeling. Sometimes we are afraid to tell others exactly how we're feeling because of a possible negative reaction. However, if in the telling we make the feeling ours, rather than something they caused, there's really nothing for them to react to. So rather than saying 'You make me feel bad', you could say 'I'm feeling bad as a result of X'. No one can deny you your feelings, so this approach is more likely to solve the problem.

Dependence

Make sure that the person you are most dependent on is yourself. If we depend on others emotionally, our happiness is quite precarious because we are effectively at the mercy of their actions. Effective relationships are a balance between giving and receiving, so if each person is 'whole' (without being dependent on the other) they can give more freely to the relationship.

Posture

Focus on correcting your posture. On a physical level, sitting and standing up straight allows your body to function efficiently. Slouching crushes the internal organs and potentially restricts bloodflow to certain areas. Sitting or standing tall gives a message of confidence that affects the responses you receive from others. Correcting your posture is likely to increase your confidence.

Learning

From now on, whenever you find yourself in an unpleasant or uncomfortable situation, ask yourself, 'What am I meant to learn from this?' or 'What is this teaching me about myself?'. If you focus on this rather than getting caught up in the unpleasantness of the situation, you will not only learn something, but you'll leave the negative emotions behind. You may even feel grateful for the learning experience.

Greener Grass

Sometimes we believe that 'the grass is greener on the other side' – if things were different, we'd be happier. The reality is that if you get to 'the other side' you will have taken your attitudes and beliefs with you. If you have the tendency to look for 'greener grass' and feel dissatisfied with your current circumstances, you'll carry this tendency with you wherever you go. But if you make the most of your current situation, you're more likely to be happy anywhere.

Strength

We all possess the strength we need to be happy in the face of whatever circumstances befall us. If someone says or does something to you that would normally upset you, know that you have all the strength you need not to be affected by it. Rather than feeling sorry for yourself, which isn't a pleasant feeling, believe that you are strong and that you can withstand anything others might say or do.

It helps to repeat the affirmation, 'I am strong and this doesn't have to affect me'.

Comfort Zones

We tend to want to stay within our comfort zones. We like to do what we've always done because we feel a sense of security in knowing what the outcome is likely to be, even when that outcome isn't positive. By doing something differently you might find that alternative outcomes are more rewarding than the ones you're accustomed to. You'll grow and learn more as you experience different ways of being. So rather than running on autopilot, try something different and notice the effects.

Self-Mastery

Remain master of yourself today. When we wake up in the morning we all want to have a good day, yet invariably things happen during the day that negatively affect our mood. This need not be the case. To remain master of yourself means deciding that today will be a good day irrespective of what happens. It's about controlling your thoughts so you only have positive ones, and controlling your behaviour rather than being influenced by others.

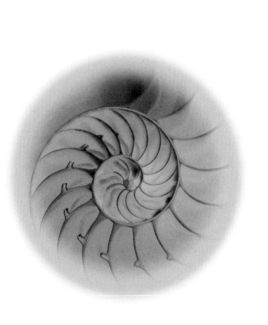

Faith

Don't expect bad things to happen.
Know that if something doesn't happen
as you expect or hope, then it was not
meant to happen that way. All
experiences come with learning
opportunities attached. It is only
through our expectations and
conditioning that we believe some
outcomes are 'good' and some are
'bad', yet this is not the case. If we let
go of our expectations and believe that
whatever happens is the best possible
outcome for the greatest learning, then
we save ourselves a lot of worry
before, during or after an event.

Appearance

Be content with your appearance because it is part of who you are. How you regard your appearance impacts on your life because how you feel about yourself will be apparent to anyone you meet. The feelings you radiate about yourself have more impact on others than your appearance. If you are happy and contented with yourself, your energy positively affects others. So make sure you don't attribute negative vibes from others to the way you look. It's more likely to be their unconscious reaction to the way you feel.

Blame

If we're not used to taking responsibility for our own feelings, we look to blame others for the way we feel, which can become a habit. There may be times when we need to talk to others about the effects of their behaviour, but the reality is that we feel the way we do as a direct result of how we think. So before slipping back into the habit of looking to someone to blame for your feelings, consider the role your own thoughts play.

Concentration

Think about your ability to concentrate. Concentration gives us the power to live in the present and be in control of our thoughts. To live in the moment we need to concentrate 100 per cent on whatever we're doing. It's possible to miss the moment by allowing the mind to drift off.

By concentrating, we can choose the thoughts we want to have, rather than letting our minds create thoughts that make us unhappy. So today, try concentrating fully on at least one thing you do and see how easy you find it. Practice will make perfect, and the results will be well worth it.

Intellect

Sometimes the intellect gets in the way of solving a problem. When faced with a problem, the brain can go into overdrive. We may try in vain to think our way out of the problem, imagining how we would handle different scenarios if this or that happened. But we'd be better off either doing something about it, or forgetting about it if it has not yet happened.

So if you catch yourself thinking obsessively about a problem, accept that no amount of thinking will solve some problems and either take action or put it aside.

Growth

If you feel as though nothing much is going right lately, or everyone seems to be on your back, consider yourself on a personal 'growth spurt'. Just as we had growth spurts when we were growing up, we can have periods of learning now. You can either feel sorry for yourself because issues are hard to deal with, or you can see it as a fantastic opportunity to come out the other side happier and with more wisdom than you have now.

Consequences

All action has consequence, whether it's good or bad, or as we intended or not. It's impossible for us to be sure about the consequence our action is going to create, but with thought and consideration we can be sure as to our intentions. If we know our actions are based on the best possible intentions, then whatever the consequence, we know we did our best. If we act without thought, or with the intention of hurting another, then we must live with the knowledge that our behaviour played a significant part in creating any negative consequences. It's far easier to modify our actions than to rectify consequences.

Perceptions

How we feel inside is far more important than what others think of us. There are times when the way we feel is at odds with others' perceptions of us. We may be doing something that makes us truly happy, but are disappointing someone in the process. Or we feel miserable inside, yet people see what we have achieved and remark how lucky or successful we are. While there are times when the two do coincide, the key thing is how you feel within yourself.

Joy

Think about the things that bring you the most joy and then try to surround yourself with them. Don't wait for these things to happen to you – dedicate time each week to making them happen!

Love

Think about someone you love. Take the time to think about why you love them and how loving them makes you feel. Also, think about how much you appreciate having them in your life and then let them know. Too often we think or feel these things but neglect to tell the person, or worse, take them for granted. By spending a little time thinking about how wonderful your loved one is and telling them about it, you'll make them feel wonderful, and you'll feel pretty good too.